This Is a Let's-Read-and-Find-Out Science Book®

HOW YOU TALK

Revised Edition

by Paul Showers • illustrated by Megan Lloyd

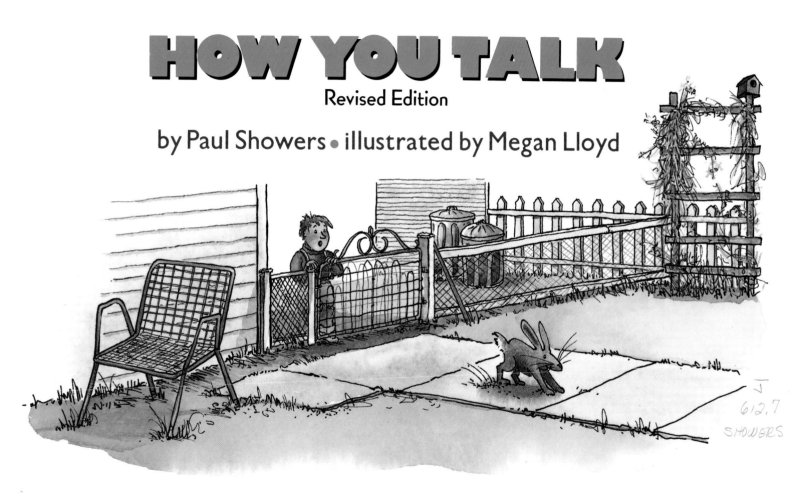

HarperCollinsPublishers

The illustrations for this book
were done in pen and ink and watercolors
on Aquarelle Arches paper.

The *Let's-Read-and-Find-Out Science Book* series was originated by Dr. Franklyn M. Branley, Astronomer Emeritus and former Chairman of the American Museum–Hayden Planetarium, and was formerly co-edited by him and Dr. Roma Gans, Professor Emeritus of Childhood Education, Teachers College, Columbia University. For a complete catalog of Let's-Read-and-Find-Out Science Books, write to HarperCollins Children's Books, 10 East 53rd Street, New York, NY 10022.

HOW YOU TALK
Text copyright © 1966, 1992 by Paul Showers
Illustrations copyright © 1992 by Megan Lloyd
Printed in the United States of America. For information address
HarperCollins Children's Books, a division of HarperCollins
Publishers, 10 East 53rd Street, New York, NY 10022.
Typography by Anahid Hamparian
1 2 3 4 5 6 7 8 9 10
Revised Edition

Library of Congress Cataloging-in-Publication Data
Showers, Paul.
    How you talk / by Paul Showers ; illustrated by Megan Lloyd. —
Rev. ed.
        p.   cm. — (Let's-read-and-find-out science book)
    Summary: Explains the mechanics of speech: what body parts are
used, and how different sounds are formed.
    ISBN 0-06-022767-2. — ISBN 0-06-022768-0 (lib. bdg.)
    1. Speech—Juvenile literature. [1. Speech.] I. Lloyd, Megan,
ill. II. Title. III. Series.
P95.S54   1992   90-1484
612.7′8—dc20   CIP
                                                     AC

My baby sister is ten months old. Her name is Kate, and she is learning to talk. No one can understand what she says. But that does not stop her. She talks all the time.

Ga-ga-ga-ga-ga

She says, "Ga-ga-ga-ga-ga."

Na-na-na-na-na

She says, "Na-na-na-na-na."

E E E E

She squeals way up high.

4

Sometimes she blows air through her lips—"Pbpbpbpb"—
or she makes a buzzing sound—"Dzzzzz."

"She's doing all right," my father says. "Don't stop her.
Kate is working hard. She is learning to make the sounds
we use when we talk."

Sue, who lives across the street, has a little brother. He is three years old. His name is Rufus, and he is learning to talk, too. Rufus talks much better than Kate. You can understand him. He can say almost anything, but he doesn't always say it right.

He can't quite say his name. He says, "My name is Wufus."

Rufus has a rabbit. His name is Benji. Rufus can say
"Benji" pretty well, but he can't say "rabbit." He calls
Benji a "wabbit."

"Never mind," Father says. "Give Rufus time to learn. He doesn't know all the ways to use his tongue. He still makes too many sounds with his lips."

9

Sue and I wanted to find out how we make sounds when we talk. You can find out, too. First, stand up and put your fingers on your chest.

LUNGS

RIBS

Feel your ribs with your fingers.
Inside your ribs are your lungs.

Close your mouth and take a deep breath. As you breathe in, your chest swells out. Air goes in your nose, down through your throat, and into your lungs. Breathe in as much as you can.

AIR

LUNGS

STOMACH

Now say, "Aaaaaaa," and let the air out s-l-o-w-l-y. Keep on saying "Aaaaaaa" as long as you can. You can say it as long as some air is in your lungs.

When you run out of air, you run out of "Aaaaaaa." You have to use your lungs when you talk.

Take another deep breath. Tip your head back and feel your throat with your fingertips. Breathe out again and say, "Aaaaaaa." Can you feel the place in your throat where the sound is made?

Ask your father to say "Aaaaaaa." Feel his throat as he says it.

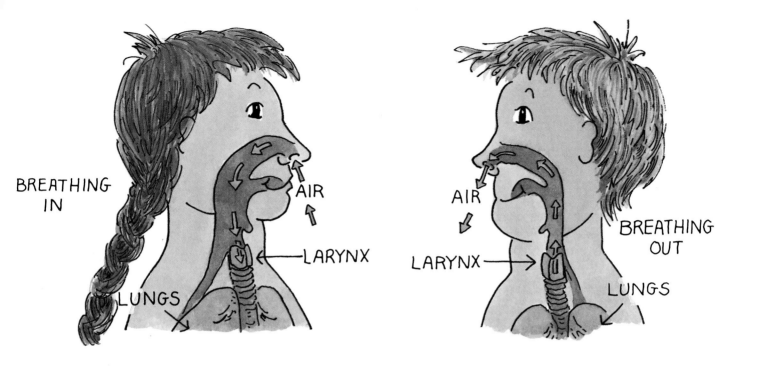

BREATHING IN

AIR

LARYNX

LUNGS

AIR

LARYNX

BREATHING OUT

LUNGS

The place where the sound is made is called the larynx. Sometimes your larynx is called your voice box. But it isn't really a box. It is a place in your throat where air goes through a narrow opening.

Air goes down through your larynx when you breathe in. It goes up through your larynx when you breathe out. Either way, you can breathe without making a sound.

14

But when you want to make a sound, when you want to
talk or sing, then you use your larynx in a special way.

Here is how your larynx works. Get a balloon and
pretend it is your lungs. Pretend the neck of the balloon is
your throat. Blow up the balloon.

Hold the neck of the
balloon shut with
both hands.

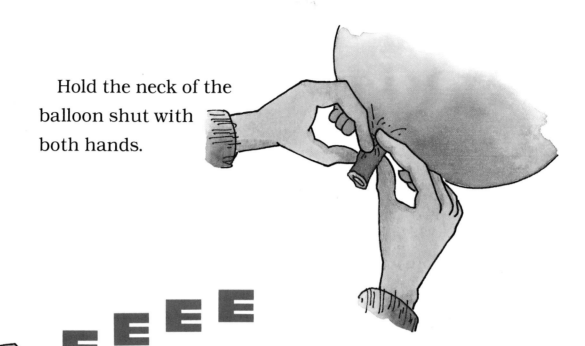

EEEE

Stretch the opening of the
balloon so that it makes
a narrow slit.

As the air comes
through the slit, it makes
a squealing sound.

If you stretch the slit to make it longer, the squeal
sounds higher.

If you make the slit shorter, the squeal sounds lower.

Your larynx works something like the slit in the balloon.
But it works much better. You use it to make all kinds of
sounds.

18

When Kate makes her funny sounds, she is learning to use her larynx. She is learning to make high sounds, low sounds, loud sounds, soft sounds.

Hold a mirror up to your mouth. Curl back your lips and show your teeth.

Open your mouth and stick out your tongue.

Tap your upper teeth with the tip of your tongue.

Make your lips round as if you were blowing out a candle.
When you talk you use your lips, your teeth, and your
tongue. You use your nose, too.

Close your mouth and hum. Keep on humming and pinch the end of your nose shut with your fingers. Let go. Now pinch it shut again.

Hmmm

Air goes through your nose when you hum. You can't hum when the air can't get through your nose.

22

DING, DING, DING

DING, DING, DING

DING, DING, DING

Pinch your nose again and say, "Ding, ding, ding." It isn't easy to say "Ding, ding, ding" when your nose is shut. You use your nose to make the sound *ng*.

Watch your mouth in the mirror and make these sounds: "Ma-aa-aa-aa." "Moo-oo-oo-oo." You change the sound when you change the shape of your lips.

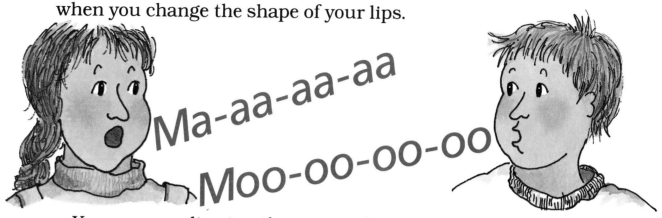

Ma-aa-aa-aa
Moo-oo-oo-oo

You use your lips in other ways when you talk. Look in the mirror and say, "Beans and bananas, butterflies and bread." Say it again slowly and watch your lips.

BEANS AND BANANAS, BUTTERFLIES AND BREAD!

Can you say these words without using your lips? Try it. Open your mouth wide. Watch your lips in the mirror. Keep them wide apart. Don't let your lips touch. Say, "Beans and bananas." Say, "Butterflies and bread." Can you do it?

Rufus uses his lips sometimes when he should use his tongue. You use your tongue when you say "Rabbits and ribbons, rockets and rope." You use your tongue for other sounds.

Try this. Open your mouth and hold down your tongue with a spoon. Say, "Rabbits and ribbons, rockets and rope." Say, "Lemons and lollipops, lizards and lace." Can you do it?

You use your teeth when you talk. Open your mouth.
Look in the mirror and say, "Thick, thin, thumbs, and
thunder." Watch how your tongue touches your upper
teeth. Say, "This, that, these, they."

People use many kinds of sounds when they talk. It takes time to learn how to make these sounds. Kate is just beginning to learn how. She can say "ga–ga–ga" but she can't say "garage." Rufus is still learning to talk. He can say "I am a big boy." But he still calls Benji a "wabbit."

Sue and I like to hear Rufus talk. He says funny things.
But we don't make fun of him. We wouldn't want to hurt
his feelings.

My father says, "Never talk baby talk to a baby. He is
doing the best he can. He is not trying to be funny. He is
just trying to talk."

When Sue and I play with Rufus, we pay no attention to
his mistakes. We help Rufus pick leaves to feed to Benji.
But we always call Benji a "rabbit." We never say "wabbit"
the way Rufus does. "Someday," my father says, "Rufus will
say 'rabbit,' too."

31